Hiroshige's
One Hundred Famous Views
of Edo

KT-416-685

YOHAN PUBLICATIONS, INC.

Note: As these postcards are slightly larger than standard size,
they require the same postage charge as first-class mail.

HIROSHIGE'S ONE HUNDRED FAMOUS VIEWS OF EDO

First edition: September 1993
Published by Yohan Publications, Inc.
14–9 Okubo 3-chome, Shinjuku-ku, Tokyo, 169 Japan

ISBN4–89684–235–9 C2071

Hiroshige's One Hundred Famous Views of Edo
The ushering in of a new age

The "One Hundred Famous Views of Edo" project was undertaken when Hiroshige was already sixty years of age and took the best part of three years to complete.

The woodblocks completed in the early stages of the series typify the "bird's eye view" tradition of Japanese prints. However, from July 1856, the perspective changed from the raised vantage point to a more immediate one, focusing more dramatically on the foreground components.

This relocation of perspective marked a radical digression from the established vertical style which Hiroshige considered inherently unsuitable for landscape prints, and indicates the inventiveness with which he tackled this limitation even into his later years.

Of the 118 preserved prints depicting Hiroshiges famous views of Edo we have chosen thirty of the most representative and trust that you will enjoy these beautiful prints of old Edo.

Ekōin Temple at Ryogōku and Moto Yanagibashi
From the series *One Hundred Famous Views of Edo*
—*Andou Hiroshige*

Kiyomizudō Temple and Shinobazu Pond at Ueno
From the series *One Hundred Famous Views of Edo*
—*Andou Hiroshige*

Hirokōji in Shitaya
From the series *One Hundred Famous Views of Edo*
—*Andou Hiroshige*

Old miniature Mt. Fuji in Megro
From the series *One Hundred Famous Views of Edo*
—*Andou Hiroshige*

Japanese Apricot garden in Kamata
From the series *One Hundred Famous Views of Edo*
—*Andou Hiroshige*

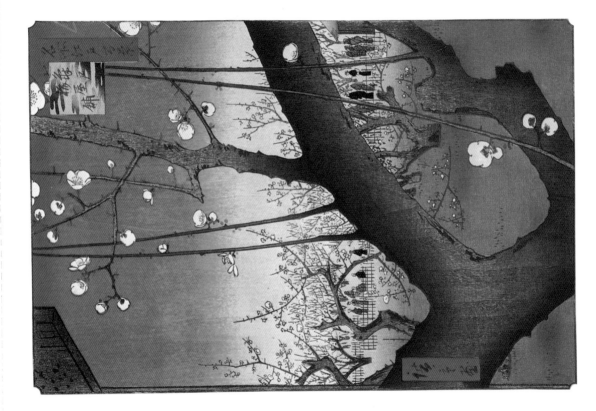

Kameido Ume (Japanese apricot) Garden
From the series *One Hundred Famous Views of Edo*
—*Andou Hiroshige*

Azuma Woods and a catalpa tree with two trunks
From the series *One Hundred Famous Views of Edo*
—*Andou Hiroshige*

Night Scene of Matsuchiyama Hill and Sanya Moat
From the series *One Hundred Famous Views of Edo*
—*Andou Hiroshige*

Matsusaki viewed from Suijin Woods on the east bank of the Sumida River
From the series *One Hundred Famous Views of Edo*
—*Andou Hiroshige*

A rough sketch of Nihonbashi-tōri 1-chōme
From the series *One Hundred Famous Views of Edo*
—*Andou Hiroshige*

A bridge having views of eight other bridges
From the series *One Hundred Famous Views of Edo*
—Andou Hiroshige

Water Supply Bridge at Suruga Terrace
From the series *One Hundred Famous Views of Edo*
—*Andou Hiroshige*

Pagoda of Zōjōji Temple and Akabane
From the series *One Hundred Famous Views of Edo*
—*Andou Hiroshige*

Tsukuda Island and Sumiyoshi Shrine Festival

From the series *One Hundred Famous Views of Edo*

—Andou Hiroshige

Thunderstorm at Ōhashi (large bridge) and Atake
From the series *One Hundred Famous Views of Edo*
—*Andou Hiroshige*

Iris flowers in Horikiri

From the series *One Hundred Famous Views of Edo*

—*Andou Hiroshige*

Kameido Tenjn Shrine grounds
From the series *One Hundred Famous Views of Edo*
—*Andou Hiroshige*

Tanabata Festival in a prospering city
From the series *One Hundred Famous Views of Edo*
—*Andou Hiroshige*

Kanda Konya-chō

From the series *One Hundred Famous Views of Edo*

—*Andou Hiroshige*

Riverside Bamboo market in Kyōbashi
From the series *One Hundred Famous Views of Edo*
—Andou Hiroshige

Kanasugi Bridge and Shiba Seashore
From the series *One Hundred Famous Views of Edo*
—*Andou Hiroshige*

Evening scene of Saruwaka-Machi
From the series *One Hundred Famous Views of Edo*
—Andou Hiroshige

*Red maple leaves, Tekona Shrine and Tsugihashi in
Mama*
From the series *One Hundred Famous Views of Edo*
—*Andou Hiroshige*

Fireworks at Ryōgoku

From the series *One Hundred Famous Views of Edo*

—*Andou Hiroshige*

Kinryūzan (temple) in Asakusa
From the series *One Hundred Famous Views of Edo*
—*Andou Hiroshige*

Ōhashi Bridge in Senju
From the series *One Hundred Famous Views of Edo*
—Andou Hiroshige

Scenery of Shiba Seashore
From the series *One Hundred Famous Views of Edo*
—*Andou Hiroshige*

Yabu Alley at the foot of Mount Atago
From the series *One Hundred Famous Views of Edo*
—*Andou Hiroshige*

Bikuni Bridge under snow
From the series *One Hundred Famous Views of Edo*
—*Andou Hiroshige*

A bird's eye view from a hilltop at Yushima
Tenjin Shrine
From the series *One Hundred Famous Views of Edo*
—Andou Hiroshige